© 2002 by Barbour Publishing, Inc.

ISBN 1-58660-423-6

Cover art: © Gettyone, Inc.

All Scripture quotations are taken from the King James Version of the Bible.

Published by Barbour Publishing, Inc., P.O. Box 719, Uhrichsville, Ohio 44683
http://www.barbourbooks.com

 Member of the
Evangelical Christian
Publishers Association

Printed in China.

CONGRATULATIONS ON YOUR ACCOMPLISHMENT

Toni Sortor

BARBOUR
PUBLISHING, INC.

diploma

Wisdom is better than rubies;
and all the things that may be desired
are not to be compared to it. . . .
I love them that love me;
and those that seek me early shall find me. . . .
For whoso findeth me findeth life,
and shall obtain favour of the LORD.

PROVERBS 8:11, 17, 35

CONGRATULATIONS!

All the long years of study are over. You are about to take your place in the world, to make your contribution, large or small, to the family of God. Education has changed you, as it should. Now it is up to you to seek wisdom, to grow into the man or woman that God plans for you to be.

. . .

Education makes people easy to lead,
but difficult to drive; easy to govern,
but impossible to enslave.

LORD BROUGHAM (1778–1868)

Let no man despise thy youth;
but be thou an example of the believers,
in word, in conversation, in charity,
in spirit, in faith, in purity.

1 TIMOTHY 4:12

KEEP LEARNING

Education does not end with a diploma. There is always something new to be learned, whether from experience or books. Now that you have graduated, you are in charge of your life. Press on with your education.

. . .

When a man's education is finished,
he is finished.

E. A. FILLENE (1860–1937)

. . .

I press toward the mark for the prize
of the high calling of God in Christ Jesus.

PHILIPPIANS 3:14

DREAM ON

Aim high. You may fall down now and then, but you will never grasp the prize if you never reach for it. Right now you may not be sure exactly what you want to do, or where, or with whom, but in time you will. You may believe your dreams are unreachable, but how will you know until you take a chance and reach out your hand to the future?

. . .

I just want to do God's will. And He's allowed me to go up to the mountain. And I've looked over, and I've seen the Promised Land.

MARTIN LUTHER KING, JR. (1929–1968)

Where there is no vision, the people perish:
but he that keepeth the law, happy is he.

PROVERBS 29:18

ENTRY-LEVEL

The most dreaded words in employment ads are "entry-level." They mean hard work, long hours, low pay, and no chance to use your brain. That's where everyone starts, where they learn the rules of work—showing up on time, being cheerful under oppression, producing on demand, and growing through it all. Once you learn the rules, you can move on to a better job. Until then, work as if you were working for God, and He will reward you.

. . .

*Nothing is really work unless you
would rather be doing something else.*

JAMES M. BARRIE (1860–1937)

. . .

But let patience have her perfect work,
that ye may be perfect and entire, wanting nothing.

JAMES 1:4

FRIENDS

The friends of our youth begin to go their own ways after graduation. Friends come and go in our lives, each making a contribution to who we are and leaving behind pleasant memories, but we have to follow our own paths, and that sometimes means leaving those we love behind. Remember that God will always guide you to appropriate new friends.

. . .

True friendship is a plant of slow growth.

GEORGE WASHINGTON (1732–1799)

. . .

A man that hath friends must shew himself friendly:
and there is a friend that sticketh closer than a brother.

PROVERBS 18:24

EMBRACING CHANGE

They hand you a diploma, say congratulations, then send you out alone into a world where everything's different. It's frightening. It's also fun. You get to make your own decisions—and live with the results. It's sort of like reinventing yourself on your own terms. Embrace change, accept responsibility, and know that God is faithfully watching your back as your life changes.

. . .

A living thing is distinguished from a dead thing by the multiplicity of the changes at any moment taking place in it.

HERBERT SPENCER (1820–1903)

. . .

For I am the Lord,
I change not. . . .

MALACHI 3:6

YOU WORKED SO HARD. . .

Getting to graduation day was not easy. . . . It involved sacrifices on your part—sacrifices of time, hard work, and the reading of a lot of books you didn't want to read. We may never have said this to you out loud, but we want you to know on this special day that we are all so proud of you!

. . .

No man who is occupied in doing a very difficult thing, and doing it very well, ever loses his self-respect.

GEORGE BERNARD SHAW (1856–1950)

And what doth the Lord require of thee,
but to do justly, and to love mercy,
and to walk humbly with thy God?

MICAH 6:8

SURROUNDED

Know that you go forth today surrounded by love, both human and heavenly. If the world treats you too harshly, you are always welcome at home or church. You are never alone. With angels ahead and behind and the love of family and friends all about you, you can overcome anything that threatens your peace. Go in love.

· · ·

Whoso loves believes the impossible.

ELIZABETH BARRETT BROWNING (1806–1861)

· · ·

There is no fear in love;
but perfect love casteth out fear.
1 JOHN 4:18

TEACHERS

You did not arrive at your graduation on your own. Behind you are twelve to sixteen years' worth of teachers who challenged you, pulled and pushed you, and put up with your nonsense because they cared for you. Within their ranks are a special two or three who really got to you—who opened your eyes, gave you a sense of direction, and made you far better than you would have been without knowing them. Say thank you whenever you can.

. . .

[Teachers], the members of the most responsible,
the least advertised, the worst paid,
and the most richly rewarded profession in the world.

IAN HAY (1876–1952)

Shew me thy ways, O Lord; teach me thy paths.
Lead me in thy truth, and teach me. . . .

PSALM 25:4–5

MIRACLES

Education teaches us to be reasonable, but those who are truly educated know that reason simply does not answer all their questions. Somewhere, somehow, there is something more at work in the world. The very young and the very old believe in miracles. So do the faithful. As you go out into the world, make room in your mind for wonder and faith and belief and the possibility of miracles in your life.

. . .

For those who believe in God no explanation is needed;
for those who do not believe in God
no explanation is possible.

FATHER JOHN LAFARGE (B. 1880)

. . .

Now faith is the substance of things hoped for,
the evidence of things not seen.

HEBREWS 11:1

WORRY

If there's one thing life soon teaches us, it's that things can go wrong, sometimes dreadfully wrong. But worrying about what might go wrong is unproductive and unhealthy. "Sufficient unto the day is the evil thereof" (Matthew 6:34). It's prudent to be cautious sometimes but foolish to be paralyzed by events that could happen. Don't let unnecessary worry hobble your daily life. God has good things in store for you!

...

Worry is interest paid on trouble before it falls due.

W. R. INGE (1860–1954)

Consider the lilies how they grow:
they toil not, they spin not;
and yet I say unto you, that Solomon in all his glory
was not arrayed like one of these.
LUKE 12:27

INDEPENDENT READING

Now that you can choose what to read, you may actually discover the true pleasure of reading. Sometimes you will read for recreation, or your tastes may run to history, science, theology, or many other categories—usually not the subject you majored in, because you're tired of that. Books are a shortcut to knowledge, leading you to wisdom (which is true education) through the lives and works of others. Anything you need to know can be found somewhere in a book.

. . .

A room without books is as a body without a soul.

SIR JOHN LUBBOCK (1834–1913)

. . .

A wise man will hear, and will increase learning;
and a man of understanding shall attain unto wise counsels.

PROVERBS 1:5

CIVILITY

You may be entering the rat race, but that doesn't mean you have to be a rat. Your success should not depend on the number of people you trample on your way to the top of the ladder. If it does, you are probably in the wrong job with the wrong company. Planning a career requires a lot of soul-searching. How much are you willing to give up to succeed? Can you get where you want while preserving your soul? Make these decisions now; don't let the marketplace make them for you.

. . .

Be nice to people on your way up because
you'll meet them on your way down.
WILSON MIZNER (1876–1933)

. . .

And be ye kind one to another,
tender hearted, forgiving one another,
even as God for Christ's sake hath forgiven you.

EPHESIANS 4:32

TRUST

Those who put their trust in this world are, sooner or later, in for disappointment. Jobs, friends, even loved ones come and go; only God is forever and worthy of total trust. Does this mean we should never trust or care for any other person? Of course not! God wants us to love others as we love ourselves, and His kingdom is a kingdom of love. Trust God first, and He will give you all the security and freedom you desire.

. . .

Set the foot down with distrust on
the crust of the world—it is thin.

EDNA ST. VINCENT MILLAY (1892–1950)

. . .

But rather seek ye the kingdom of God;
and all these things shall be added unto you.

LUKE 12:31

CHARACTER

Suppose that no one, not even God, knew everything you did in your life, the good and the bad. No one observed you shunning the poor or giving to the poor. No one heard your harsh words or your compassionate ones. No one knew your deepest thoughts and beliefs. Suppose what you did was totally hidden from others. How would you live with such freedom, with no fear of punishment for your bad acts and no reward for your good ones? The way you would live in this situation is your character, the true you. Can you live with that person?

. . .

Character is what you are in the dark.
DWIGHT MOODY (1837–1899)

. . .

Giving all diligence, add to your faith virtue;
and to virtue knowledge; and to knowledge temperance;
and to temperance patience; and to patience godliness;
and to godliness brotherly kindness;
and to brotherly kindness charity.

2 PETER 1:5–7

CHARITY

We tend to think we can show our charity by the simple act of writing a few checks each year, but charity is so much more. It is a way of life, of giving of ourselves, of loving all of God's creation, especially when it's hard, and of taking no credit for what we do. Fortunately for the world, young people seem to understand this better than their elders, perhaps because their lives are less cluttered and they live in closer proximity to poverty. Keep charity in your heart forever.

. . .

The biggest disease today is not leprosy or tuberculosis, but rather the feeling of being unwanted.

MOTHER TERESA (1911–1997)

. . .

And now abideth faith, hope, charity, these three;
but the greatest of these is charity.

1 CORINTHIANS 13:13

CONFESSION

As we grow older, we find more things to confess. A little child will smack another, both will cry a little, then go back to playing with no remorse. Adults can't get away with that. If the other does not hit back, then our conscience will. Adults say "I'm sorry," and if they are smart they will mean it. Don't belabor your sins; confess them and rest assured that they will be forgiven.

. . .

We have left undone those things which we ought to have done;
and we have done those things which we
ought not to have done.

BOOK OF COMMON PRAYER

. . .

I prayed unto the Lord my God,
and made my confession, and said, O Lord. . .
we have sinned, . . .and have done wickedly. . . .

DANIEL 9:4–5

CHURCH

Now that you have graduated and moved out of your parents' house, who will wake you in time for church? Whether you will attend or not is now your responsibility. Don't be put off just because you don't feel "good enough" to join the pillars of society in worship. Pillars are under as much pressure as you are, and sometimes they shake, too.

. . .

The Church after all is not a club of saints;
it is a hospital for sinners.

GEORGE CRAIG STEWART (1870–1940)

. . .

This is a faithful saying, and worthy of all acceptation,
that Christ Jesus came into the world to save sinners;
of whom I am chief.
1 TIMOTHY 1:15

PROBLEMS

The problems of a child are usually overcome by dinner and a good night's sleep, but problems seem to multiply as we get older and perhaps wiser. No one escapes all of life's problems; the trick is deciding how to face them and working to change them from threats to opportunities.

. . .

*When written in Chinese the word "crisis" is
composed of two characters.
One represents danger and the other represents opportunity.*

JOHN F. KENNEDY (1917–1963)

Be ye strong therefore, and let not your hands be weak:
for your work shall be rewarded.

2 CHRONICLES 15:7

HANDLING MONEY

Handling money properly has two sides: spending and saving. We all know how to spend. A child can do it. But when it comes to saving, we often have to learn the hard way. Sitting down with your check-book and seeing exactly where your money is going may be boring and frustrating, but it's better than ending up broke at the end of the month and unable to pay the rent.

. . .

Live within your income.
Always have something saved at the end of the year.
Let your imports be more than your exports,
and you'll never go far wrong.

DR. SAMUEL JOHNSON (1709–1784)

. . .

He becometh poor that dealeth with a slack hand:
but the hand of the diligent maketh rich.
PROVERBS 10:4

"EXPERIENCE REQUIRED"

If you've never had a job or can't get a job, how are you to ever become experienced in any field? It's a Catch-22 thing. But unless you've lived alone in a cave for the last eighteen years, you do have experience. You've had part-time or summer jobs; you've baby-sat for your brothers and sisters; you've helped in the fields; you know how to run computer programs. Whatever you have done that shows your willingness to work, your ability to show up on time every day, can be phrased as experience on your first resumé. Take whatever you have done and turn it into an experience.

. . .

Experience is not what happens to a man.
It is what a man does with what happens to him.

ALDOUS HUXLEY (1894–1963)

. . .

We glory in tribulations also:
knowing that tribulation worketh patience;
and patience, experience; and experience, hope.

ROMANS 5:3–4

DECISIONS

It's impossible to please everyone and foolish to try. Life is full of decisions—some big and some small—and eventually you will be faced with choosing and living with the consequences of your choice. Rest assured that God will help you make the right decisions and comfort you when others disagree with the path you have chosen.

. . .

I cannot give you the formula for success,
but I can give you the formula for failure—
which is: Try to please everybody.

HERBERT B. SWOPE (1882–1958)

. . .

Because thou hast been my help,
therefore in the shadow of thy wings will I rejoice.

PSALM 63:7

PARENTS

Teens go through a period when nothing their parents do pleases them. They seem so out of step, stuck in some prehistoric time called "When I was your age." Then the children go off on their own and discover that their parents were right a good deal of the time. Patience and respect are needed on both sides because no generation is right all of the time, and every generation has something to teach the generation that follows.

. . .

When I was a boy of fourteen, my father was so ignorant
I could hardly stand to have the old man around.
But when I got to be twenty-one,
I was astonished at how much he had learned in seven years.

MARK TWAIN (1835–1910)

. . .

A wise son heareth his father's instruction:
but a scorner heareth not rebuke.

PROVERBS 13:1

THE RESULTS OF KINDNESS

Not everyone is able to change the whole world through direct personal action. Our problems are too complex to expect that. But everyone is capable of changing the world a little, one person at a time. Being polite when harshness is expected can cause another to choose politeness over anger. No one knows the daily acts of kindness this world benefits from, but they are invaluable.

. . .

That best portion of a good man's life,
His little, nameless, unremembered acts
Of kindness and love.

WILLIAM WORDSWORTH (1770–1850)

. . .

Put on therefore, as the elect of God,
holy and beloved, bowels of mercies, kindness,
humbleness of mind, meekness, longsuffering.

COLOSSIANS 3:12

28

RAIN

We all get caught out in the rain now and then. No one escapes getting wet because of his religious beliefs. In the same way, even the best of us suffer from sickness, sadness, heartbreak, and death. It's how we deal with life's common problems that distinguishes the faithful from the unfaithful. Praise God in all circumstances, and if it rains on you, it's time to plant a garden.

. . .

Thy fate is the common fate of all;
Into each life some rain must fall.

HENRY WADSWORTH LONGFELLOW (1807–1882)

For he maketh his sun to rise on the evil and on the good,
and sendeth rain on the just and on the unjust.

MATTHEW 5:45

29

GREATNESS

A truly great person is considered great because he or she knows how to make others feel extraordinary. A great person sees the good in those around him and brings out even more of their talents. He cheers them on when things are difficult, helps them love their enemies, and brings God's mercy into their lives.

. . .

The really great man is the man who
makes every man feel great.

G. K. CHESTERTON (1874–1936)

. . .

I say unto you, Love your enemies,
bless them that curse you,
do good to them that hate you, . . .and persecute you.

MATTHEW 5:44

PRIORITIES

Before you can help others, you have to get your own priorities in order, because actions always follow beliefs. Wicked people can do good deeds now and then, but they can't sustain these actions for very long. It's like trying to smile when there is no happiness in you; it gets tiring. If you would do good, know what you believe and act on your beliefs.

. . .

Men are not made religious by
performing certain actions which are eternally good,
but they must first have righteous principles,
and then they will not fail to perform virtuous actions.

MARTIN LUTHER (1484–1546)

. . .

I put on righteousness, and it clothed me:
my judgment was as a robe and a diadem.

JOB 29:14

WISDOM

You don't have to be highly educated to be wise. Education is necessary and valuable, but it's only one part of wisdom. We all know people with little formal education who are extremely wise. They have a grasp of what is truly important in life and live lives of grace and wisdom. Formal education will cease; seeking wisdom is a life's work.

. . .

*I have never let my schooling
interfere with my education.*

MARK TWAIN (1835–1910)

. . .

Happy is the man that findeth wisdom,
and the man that getteth understanding.

PROVERBS 3:13

CONFIDENCE

Remember the confidence you feel today on your graduation. The whole world is at your feet—there is nothing you cannot accomplish. God knows and loves you. All of this is true and worthy of celebration. If you would do great things in your life, you need this self-confidence. Don't let anyone steal it away from you. Remember this day and know your confidence comes from God, your protector and guide.

. . .

Self-confidence is the first requisite to great undertakings.

DR. SAMUEL JOHNSON (1709–1784)

For the LORD shall be thy confidence,
and shall keep thy foot from being taken.

PROVERBS 3:26

SUFFERING

We are human; we suffer. Sometimes we know the source of our suffering, but often we don't. We get the flu; we struggle to feed ourselves and our family; we grow sick and die. Whatever our faith, life has its bad times. Jesus, the only Son of God, suffered for us as an example of both how to live and how to die. His faith never wavered. May yours remain strong as you meet the common difficulties of us all.

. . .

God had one son on earth without sin,
but never one without suffering.

SAINT AUGUSTINE (354–430)

. . .

For even hereunto were ye called:
because Christ also suffered for us,
leaving us an example, that ye should follow his steps.

1 PETER 2:21

TEACHING

It's amazing what one good teacher can do. Say he or she really reaches four students a year, changing them into eager learners with purpose. Over a career of forty years, that one teacher has forever changed the lives of 160 students. How many people can claim that much influence in the world?

. . .

A teacher affects eternity.

HENRY B. ADAMS (1838–1918)

. . .

Warning every man, and teaching every man in all wisdom;
that we may present every man perfect in Christ Jesus.

COLOSSIANS 1:28

HARD TIMES

Hard times often isolate us. We don't want others to know we're treading the thin line between "getting by" and all-out poverty. We pull ourselves into the fortress of home, button it up, and hope to ride the wave back to sufficiency. Pride isolates us from people more than willing to help, even from God. When times are hard, have the faith to go out into the world and help those in even more trouble. Trust in the Lord and He will not fail you.

. . .

It's a recession when your neighbor loses his job;
it's a depression when you lose yours.

HARRY S. TRUMAN (1884–1972)

. . .

For want and famine they were solitary;
fleeing into the wilderness. . .

JOB 30:3

FELLOWSHIP

You know you are maturing when you start saying "we" more than "I."
The "we" may be you and someone you love, a special group of
friends, a family, or a country. There's a bond between you that has
meaning, and you care for these people deeply. You sacrifice for them
and they for you. You have learned the value of fellowship.

. . .

*One of the signs of passing youth is the birth of
the sense of fellowship with other human beings
as we take our place among them.*

VIRGINIA WOOLF (1882–1941)

. . .

If we walk in the light, as he is in the light,
we have fellowship one with another,
and the blood of Jesus Christ his Son cleanseth us from all sin.

1 JOHN 1:7

MERCY

There are times when we are at the mercy of others and times when we have the upper hand. What shows the true character of a person is not only how he suffers under adversity but how he acts when he has the advantage. The merciful shall receive mercy. Those who pass up the advantage are stronger than those who take revenge.

. . .

Next to knowing when to seize an opportunity,
the most important thing in life is to know
when to forego an advantage.

BENJAMIN DISRAELI (1804–1881)

. . .

The wicked borroweth, and payeth not again:
but the righteous sheweth mercy, and giveth.

PSALM 37:21

THE LIVING GOD

There are dead gods and the living God. The first offer us nothing because they are forever stuck in the past, unable to relate or respond to our real needs. But the living God is the God of all ages and circumstances, still working His will and building His kingdom through His love for us. When the time comes—and it will—for you to choose, choose the living God.

. . .

To believe in God for me is to feel that there is a God,
not a dead one or a stuffed one, but a living one,
who with irresistible force urges us toward more loving.

VINCENT VAN GOGH (1853–1890)

. . .

My soul thirsteth for God, for the living God.

PSALM 42:2

LEAVING HOME

You have to go. It's time to leave the comfort of home and build your own life. Be aware that this is a difficult time for your parents. They are so proud of what you have accomplished and will accomplish, but letting you go is the hardest thing they will ever do. Stay in touch. Go with God.

. . .

Selfhood begins with a walking away,
And love is proved in the letting go.

C. DAY LEWIS (1904–1972)

. . .

Therefore shall a man leave his father and his mother. . . .

GENESIS 2:24